GETTING HERE

GETTING HERE

FRED WEINER

LARSON PUBLICATIONS

International Standard Book Number: 0-943914-91-4

Library of Congress Catalog Card Number: 98-67554

Published by

Larson Publications

4936 NYS Route 414

Burdett, New York 14818 USA

05 04 03 02 01 00 99

10 9 8 7 6 5 4 3 2 1

for my wife and son

dull-witted, I sit
scratching my pen on this sheet
surprised at the words

—∞∞∞—

rumble of the bus
my son three thousand miles gone
once, his tiny feet

—∞∞∞—

banging, banging again
the cardinal
at the window

the way the violet dawn entered the tent with its coolness
the way I knew the day's darkness when I awoke
the braying of the asses in the cold
the way his body lay on the straw in the cold light of dawn
the way he stirred and came awake
the way the sweetness in his gaze disarmed me
the way we looked in each other's faces to kindle laughter
the way I came to know our destination
the wail of Ishmael when he saw me
the way my father led me into light
the way the men spoke in low tones around him
the way their deference felt quiet in my body
the radiance of his brow, the depth of his thought
the silence at the morning meal, the bitterness of the herbs
the way the women stayed in the shadows
the way he took up the fire
the way I carried the fire and the knife
the way the ass walked under her load
the remorseless ascending sun
the rough stones under my feet, the harsh wood on
    my back, the dust and the sweat

the way I drank the water in its time
the way I knew gratitude, and the nothingness of thirst
the way bitterness came upon me as I saw the hill
the way the wood bore into my back as I took the hill
the way he walked with me, carrying fire
my wonder at the absence of the lamb
the way I said the time had come
the way I took him and bound him and laid him up
    to sacrifice
the way he said he feared me not, but was afraid
the way I knew the nothingness in my heart
the way the knife edge blazed with holy fire
the way we were revealed to each other
the way the Deep Wisdom informed me in its purpose
and I came to know he belonged to God alone
the way the ram came in its time for the offering
the sudden coolness in the breeze
the red blood, the stillness

air thick with moisture
the pond cold from last night's rain
at the shoreline, frogs

———✖———

elegant curved arms—
mahogany rocker sits
unused in the room

———✖———

a fountain
in the heart
and yet—thirst

THE CALL

The way the sun moves south this time of year,
leaving us in darker rooms, the plants crying
softly to themselves, I feel the coming
of the cold and dark days; they rise up
to greet me first in memory, hardly noticeable,
until a morning with cold dew on the lawn
finds me with numb toes and a shiver of tension
wrapped around my spine; then I start testing
my breath against the air, still invisible,
look for Orion in the night sky, still too early,
and a hot muggy day interposes itself
and I forget again. Dreams of an icy lake
and a girl drowning under the flows, and me
diving to save her, not feeling the cold at all,
come to me while Andromeda still traverses
the deep night sky, chained and waiting
for her hero to come, and again I imagine
the winter landscapes, this time with me absent,
somewhere where the south-heading sun
still has the strength to warm me. Passing
from dream to wakefulness, from imagination
to this room in late summer, resounding
with a booming chorus of cicadas, I remember
that I save her by listening not to the cold
voice of fear in me, but to the call.

sunrise
without sound—
fireball in the trees

—Ω—

after days of dry heat
the whisper of rain
on wisteria leaves

—Ω—

last time she kissed me
she put her hand in my shirt
fondled my nipple

ONE MOON

one moon
a few rinds
of Spanish tangerine
cast in the azure sea

and so much sunlight
glinting and twinkling
in the masts
of the sailing ships;

the swell,
the lift and fall
in my breast,
the dying onshore breeze;

O Moorish girl—
framed in the archway
of my whitewashed room—
dark eyes shimmering—
raven locks
at your shoulders—
smile for me

sickle moon
rising huge at the top of the road
frightens me

———⚬⚬⚬———

her scent, like horses
moves me to insanity—
married another

———⚬⚬⚬———

like jewels
the dewdrops
on broccoli leaves

deep in the horse trough
the green frog swims frantically
trying to escape

——

the sound
beneath the breeze
no sound

——

I look at the clock—
six twenty-two, time to go.
Now—six forty-nine!

I saw you stand at the top of the field
Close by the pine we had just dug in,
Nurturing it by being there;
Did your soundless voice say *hear* or *here?*

bring the water bucket
hear the sibilant wind
join me blessing

this sacred site with sound
bring the bucket here
aspire with heart and hand
to honor the hallowed land

I said, *I will.*
I climbed the hill
To your spot in the field.
The water bucket, half-filled
In the roadside stream
Rubbing my pants-leg seam
In time with my pace.
I reached your place.

your feet had merged with the earth;
your eyes saw far as the stars.

I bent to pour water on the flattened ground
Where you had tamped the dirt around
The seedling pine with your feet.
The water seeped down through the peat
To reach the root.

I wonder, *did Ariadne play the lute*
for Theseus, before she gave the thread
that led him from the monster to her bed?

I straightened up to see the scudded sky
Reflected in the greenness of your eye.
You hadn't moved.
The ground, the hill, the sky seemed soothed.
We two stood in that field, felt blessed
By the quiet that moves in sounds, to quietness.

silence
except for the birds
except for the sunrise

remembering
what it's like to be a nun
brushing my hair

white tails thrust upward
bounding across frozen ground
the Autumn-fat deer

HOMAGE TO ALLEN GINSBERG

(June 3, 1926 – April 5, 1997)

Hail to thee, fire in the West, thousand armed one,
Ferocious against repression of truth, destroyer of
The heart's bondage, liberator, wrathful energy provider,
Harvester of skulls, of impure hearts, devourer of
    afflicted brains,
Liver eater, bowel exploder, thou, fanged with flaming swords:
Bless him who has now come home to thee, suppliant,
    to whom
You gave a portion of your fire, who laughed at
    embarrassment,
Who took it in the ass for thy pleasure, who sucked cum
Ten thousand times for thy nourishment, who echoed the best
Of his progenitors in the race of poets, in whom you founded
A generation of thinkers and doers toiling to be true to
    themselves,
Who with his last breaths did honor thee still, who for
    a moment
Saw deep into his nature and was dazzled there by thee,
Who honors us, the lowest and vilest part as honorable as
    the noblest,
Free we are as one, and free we are intertwined with
    many forms
Of our choosing, free as he is free in thy terrible, thy
    loving peace,
AUM

morning sun diamondsparkle snowfield:
blackbirds

※

crows, so many crows
gather by scores on the road
fly away screaming

※

cat on the chair-back
purring loud into my ear
claws in my shoulder

BREAKING ICE FOR THE HORSES

snow covers most of the pasture now:
dead shoots from the late summer grasses,
something of the sun's gold still in them,
wave in the wind and the whole scene
is defined in lines of stark white and the gold
and the reddish tinge in the hedgerow:
the pale blue of dawn is already deepening
in the sky: the shovel sends sparks
into the ice as it strikes stone:
a thin rivulet of water runs across
the top of the icy trench:
hammering at it with the sharp edge of the shovel,
the edge eventually breaks through—
slush sound: indeed, there's still water
running under there despite the cold:
hacking out two-inch thick pieces of ice:
now throwing them aside upstream, out of the way:
it runs muddy at first, then clears:
calling them, they look up, but continue
at their hay: I get it: they'll find
the water when they need to
like they always do—I'm the one
who has to dig for it

as if
out of nowhere
the bluejay

———❧———

in the cafe
taking icing from her cake
she's alert to my moves

———❧———

even with the sun
and clear sky and birds
sad morning

HEARING YOUR POEM

In the old Chinese paintings
a few strokes is all it took
to show a mountain range.
Usually there's a footbridge;
a tiny figure stands part way
across. The moment captured
combines vastness and the mundane
so seamlessly that the impression
is of fathomless emptiness
behind everything. "From the first,
not a thing is," says sage Hui Neng.

Hearing your poem, I feel myself
motionless on that bridge,
suddenly, momentarily, momentously
a part of everything. When I allow,
I feel the water moving
beneath my sandaled feet,
remember that my staff just clattered
on the creaking boards.
In that instant, even the water
is mere potential. I might as well
not have a body, for all
I perceive of it, or my body
might as well be everything.
Your meaning is there,
timeless as the hills.

light rain
puckers the pond's
smooth surface

━━✖━━

the phone
jangling me awake—
it's her

━━✖━━

the jay's harsh laugh
before he steals
catfood

BY WATER

Log-scent and log-sound on the fast river
jammed two miles past the glistening fork
above Wachahatchie, lumbermen come down
to inspect it all. Must've confounded the beavers
back behind the brakes; we thought we heard
their thumping now and then above the din.

Clear cold nights are coming fast; the stars
more brilliant now the sun is moving south.
Woodsmoke drifting on evening air puckers
the nose. Remember when it all seemed so new,
like the time we loaned Rachel the car
and stayed alone in the cabin days on end.

Light fading, the frogs trying their best
to outlast the human race, the way they're
wailing at each other by the water's edge.
Summers ago, I saw you swimming here
sunburned as a ripe peach, water dripping
from your flanks as you climbed onto the bank
naked, laughing at me crouching under hemlocks.

coming up for air
I'm face to face
with a dragonfly

—⊛—

hind end destroyed
thrashing in the roadside ditch—
yearling fawn

—⊛—

after the rain
leaves dripping on the deck
cooing of the doves

PASSOVER

The Angel of Death passes over
They have marked their doorways with Lambsblood
Trembling inside, they waited
Soon the streets resound with the Wailing of Mothers
Horror and Gratitude show by torchlight
In the grim faces of Householders spared the slaughter
Watching the Mothers clutching dead children to their breasts
Some feel the Responsibility they have been given
Their Descendants dedicate themselves to Truth
Others feel Relief and Compassion
Their Descendants dedicate themselves to Love of their Families
Others feel Superiority and Gloating
Their Descendants perish by Poison and Fire
A nation is forming with this complexity of feeling
They wander in search of a Home
Their Restlessness carries them onward
Across the Desert and Many Lands
Carrying the mark of Victim in their breasts
One day there came a Redeemer
Showing the way to the Heart
We have failed to heed Him
Today we slaughter Ourselves
Our Doorways are marked by Blood
The Festivals fail to remove it
Be Gentle with Yourselves, He said
Forgive Yourselves, He said
Forgive the Others, He said
Then You'll no longer be enslaved

The cliff face behind me, my place is on this rock,
Coal black in the rain. Icebergs straddle the horizon.
Ships enter the icy bay from the Southwest.
Something is wrong but I can't tell what it is.
Lately I've been having dreams and visions while awake.
Their messages confuse me. I must give up trying
To know everything. I must wash my hair and anoint
    my head
With oil from last year's hunting. Only the long days
Keep me from entering that endless sleep that beckons me.
Here and there the cormorants break the heaving surface
Of the sea. Overhead gulls call me Eastward where the sun
Rides a low gray cushion of sky. Soon the rain will come
Again, washing the bits and pieces into the ground
And over the rocks. The heart knows where it's going.

The Fathers had declared the season over, still the hunters
Were on the sea. The Right-whale had returned to
    these waters.
Niwannanguk speared two Narwhal. The Fathers knew
    the season
Was over. I hailed them from the land spit as they returned.
My clothes were newly made from the village. Niwannanguk
Recognized me by my hair. He beckoned me to his boat
For the blubber. I tasted with him when the cutting began.
We talked of long journeys, his in the sea, mine in dreams.

I saw him there the hunter of Walrus, Narwhal, Beluga,
    Right-whale.
His speartip red in the black sky, his eyes aflame.
Beckoning in the dream, the black without stars.
High his kayak rode the waves, deep the troughs, but no wind.
Sounds of the sea creatures singing his name. His companion
The gray wave tips. Up came Beluga to receive his spear.

I called him to me after the hunt. We lay together,
The furs parted. Now the pleasure of the Fathers, the Mothers.
We shall be declared Two-As-One from this day onward.
Fathers Mothers Sisters Brothers Cousins Uncles Aunts
Declare us One with them. Out to sea, a Right-whale blows.
Light comes from the ice; my furs warm me. Onward rides
    the sun.

I'm a violin
strings plucked by angels and ghosts
the music is mine

———∞∞∞———

changing to snow tires—
cold wet grease on the lug nuts
turns my fingers black

———∞∞∞———

my hunger for her
again

TRANSITION

So the light is fine, soft,
Suffused with burnt orange,
As if the dying sun had fired
The last clouds of the day
Just for us.

Gradually, I'm
Losing my ability to lie.
You must understand
How much it means to me.

I have no hands to shape things
In the fire. I want to touch ground,
Trembling, the fire in my eyes.

when death comes
will I be awake
to this?

—❦—

such a quiet rain
reminds me of my childhood
staying indoors . . .

—❦—

her husband's old car
parked in the field close to mine
under a half moon

WALKING

Walking across the asphalt parking lot
along the busy city street and beneath
the underpass, the smell of diesel reminds me
of London, and the time we cheered each other
walking, in spite of the rain, in spite of
the suitcases, anticipation blending with the simple
comfort of being together so far from home.

Something intrigues me about the concrete steps
on the far side of the underpass leading up
from the roadway beneath the bridge to the roadway
above: forethought of road engineers to include
a passageway for pedestrians, but did they reckon
on trolls, or the magic of ascending to an upper
level on one's own power? The steps are a little
short on the rise, so I stumble near the top,
catching myself on the cold metal railing painted
industrial green. Smooth sailing from here on,
across the upper road and beyond, into the sweet
autumn sunlight and brightly colored air, passing
through crowds of beautiful young girls and lean
athletic men, not a single one of them noticing
how desperately I long to be with you.

dancing past midnight
too drunk on beer to slow down
today, disaster

standing at the sink
scrubbing out the garbage pail
the smell not quite gone

hiding
behind my eyes
sorrow

THE BREATH

The circle the breath makes stops the heart.
Crows calling from the outside
levitate the mood a bit, such rascals.
Sobering to think they'd eat your eyeballs.
But there is a kinship, if only the winged part.
Left to their own devices, they leave us to ours.
More than I can say for the stones,
always insinuating themselves under foot.
But then, what is "inanimate" anyway?
The closing of a book, lights out, alone under stars.
The breath is all there is between you and them.

I

I'll taste
what only you have felt
in the dark
in secret.

II

Never
have your lips been closer
than this time.

III

Limbs crack from the trees
no one hears
no one sees
the storm tossed pines.

IV

Soft rain,
thunder,
the place where you are.

V

Loose in your fields
a red wolf.

VI

Your dark eyes
swimming in darkness—
my heart.

VII

In the stream
back behind your house
a sliver moon.

VIII

Sexual longing,
peace in the heart—
I can't tell
the difference.

IX

The time
you touched me
just that way—
I wept.

X

You lift your arm,
let your legs rest open—
I'm lost.

XI
Locked in your room
a love drunk madman
no escape.

XII
How sharp
the face
of your cat.

XIII
Did you think of me
when the rains came—
eaves dripping like tears.

XIV
When the world is wet
and warm like this
the longing deepens.

XV
Just when I feel
everything is lost—
your smile.

XVI
The air so moist
it's almost wet—
drunk on peonies.

XVII
No separation
yet,
your perfume . . .

BLOOD IN THE DESERT

Today I'm waiting for the mood to pass
Like the thickening layer of strato-cumulus
Sliding across the sun from the north,
Or the rippling breeze that, for the 28th time
This week, makes me wish I'd brought my sweatshirt;
My arm's all goose-pimply and it's too sensitive
Underneath the cotton shirt. Twelve nights
Of spilling myself into the dark loamy places
Of my fragile, my errant wife, have left
Me heatless in the desert. I go to piss
Behind the mesquite beyond the twin steel-cabled
Parking lot fence and learn another lesson
About appropriate footwear where everything
Underfoot is sharp and pointed at tender instep flesh
Sandled for safer terrain. Rose-dark drops rise along
A thin red line and shimmer, like fresh boys
Pouring out over the tops of their trenches

Oblivious to death. The piss stream spews
From its fleshy hydrant, spatters on hard
Quartzite-strewn ground and pelts my legs
On the rebound. Back in the car she's looking
At the slides she took when her presence
Behind the camera lit the panorama of flower
Tree and sky as if the sun had ignited
Her limbering body on that snow-sheeted mountain.
Today her dusky blood channels earthward with
The rhythm of the moon, full last night and casting
Pearl-light through the half-drawn blinds
On her teardrop-shaped bottom and the bedsheets
While I looked on, lost in the breath of rapture.
What the blood carries from darkness into deeper
     darkness
Is like the single, thorn-sheared, blood red rose
She holds while tears of gratitude and sorrow
Flood her face, and the whole span of anxious waiting
Culminates in the uncertain destiny of a flower.

ice in the buckets
some of my houseplants are gone—
too late to save them

---

pink cottony clouds
the great dome of the dawn sky—
I limp toward the pond

---

so soft
her belly under my tongue,
her sighs

AT DELPHI

it seemed impossible
making the rough climb
the Aegean a blue haze
under bone white sky,
Parnassus' broad back looming:
by now my question
sounded deeper than name or body—
the jagged rocks under my feet
felt almost soothing
compared to *that* penetration—
only doubt remained,
thin as the scorching air,
between me and her presence

it was there with her
squatting on the rock,
her black hair flying,
wild eyes staring at nothing,
it was there
in her guttural, uncadenced speech,
there
in the hot wind hissing in the cypresses—
even in the garbled muttering of the priests—
the answer:
rising in my body now like venom
setting my brain afire
ineffable
surpassing even sorrow with truth

CUSHION

Once it might have been
part of a favorite TV room chair,
something to sink into;
now it lies rotting at the curbside,
upholstery in tatters moldering to black,
rusting springs thrusting into the gaps.

No chance for us to sit on it
and have a conversation.
The rusting springs pose danger enough;
laundering the rot would be a nightmare,

like the writhing thing I saw
on the wet black asphalt
driving home: I sucked in breath
at some primordial, harm avoiding urge.
The breath stuck in my chest awhile,
reminding of the heart. It turned out
to be a pine branch rolling in the wind.

We might try to sit on this compulsion
to let words stand in for the body,
rolling phalanxes of words piled high
into towers; words, phrases, sentences
become vast sprawling buildings
mushrooming into cities, nations of words
shouting down the black bottom root silence
where pain lies waiting, throats parched
as the grass on dry season savanna, gasping
in dust blown across the broken face of the moon.

Let's sit on this compulsion.
What feels like a pain in the ass
is life caressing
what we no longer feel
we need to protect.

remembering, forgetting—
still, the undertow . . .

—◦◦◦—

all this sadness—
such a perfect day
for rain

—◦◦◦—

waiting for thunderstorms
even the high elm branches
are still

LOVE IN THE COLD

Five maple leaves I take from the carpet
Of flames spreading across the yard
Thinking to send them to her in Arizona,
A reminder of the deciduous rhythm
Of green, and green dying to fire;

Like the spider, a speckled globus in
Her ancient patterned orb, motionless
Buddha astride her silk-wrapped nourishing fly,
Her meditation on sustenance and killing, both;

Or how the family dog refuses to come in
Barking at some ghosts at the end
Of the driveway, leaving a hollow space
In my throat from calling in the cold;

Or opening a door on lovers unawares
Whose eyes, vacant with intimacy, turn
To glimpse the unrecognizable intruder, their
Solitary whispers pulsing in my ears;

The coughing fit that stands in place of weeping,
The sidelong glances toward the hidden place
Of pain and shadowed darkness worth the keeping,
A blaze of light regarded face to face.

MY FIRST TRIP TO FLORIDA

FOR DAD ON HIS SEVENTY-THIRD BIRTHDAY

You drove   the two-toned-blue fifty-eight Pontiac
with fins and dual headlights   power steering
that big power brake pedal   our first trip to Florida
past Greensburg Hagerstown Fredricksburg Richmond
Durham Fayetteville Charleston Savannah   the Ludowici
                                        speed trap
and the one at Jessup   by Jacksonville the sides of the
                    highway
had become so green   counting license plates from each state
your shining head clean above the seat   your face in profile
your mouth a thin line a smile a faint frown   leaned so
                                        far left
shoulder against the door   (I secretly held it closed with
                    my worry)
left arm resting on the door   against the closed window
hand on the steering wheel at ten o'clock   I could see the
                                        thick fingers
the light brown hairs in the sections   between the knuckles
the gold band that must have clicked the wheel   when you
                                        gripped
the peeling palm against the wheel   it must have felt good
the road hum through the wheel   the right arm at your side
its hand holding the wheel at five o'clock   or arm and
                                        hand resting
across the top of the seatback   fingertips touching
                    mother's shoulder

or swinging the whole thing behind you   to swat at us
                                        like flies
when we were boisterous or bored   torturing our sister
or singing too loud   mother's warnings about restrooms
dirty toilet seats in old gas stations   along the way
roastbeefsandwiches browngravy whitebread mashedpotatoes
hamburgers and frenchfries   glasses of milk or pepsi
pancakes in restaurants adjacent to motels   mornings along
                                        the way
until we saw the first palm trees   felt the moisture in the
                                hot air
blowing our faces through open windows   until we entered
                                        the streets
of Miami where you knew   where to make the turns
                        unfailingly
how you showed your excitement   by greater focus
and the slightest smile   how we arrived at the little house
with an open carport   and lawn of the thickest grass
it felt like stepping on sponges   and a gardenia hedge
a cracked front sidewalk   and Pappy's arms across his chest
waiting for us   and Daisy growling and chasing herself
                in circles
and we're running, running   and Mammy's cackling
                        laughter

Spring morning
floortiles cold
in the bathroom

—∞—

the cat on hind legs
drinking from the roof-drip pail—
last week's snow

—∞—

if only this rain
could wash away
the sadness

POOR POET

In the room with the jade-tile floor
You order me to undress
In the sequence you have discovered.
I am a poor poet in your court.
You give the orders.

In the desert of Turkestan,
Traveling after dusk to avoid the heat,
The camels know the way.
Yours is the only moisture for miles,
And I drink deeply.
The crossing is not a hardship.

LIGHT IN THE DINING ROOM

Light in the dining room is greener in June;
The lilacs and maple fully leafed out filter it,
The two south windows and the southeast transmit it
With the quality of emerald or jade
Imparted to it like a benediction.

The room feels blessed, and the candle I light—
To soften the dark place in me that has contracted
To a singular darkness like a melanoma, or an inkstain
On white paper like the kind on which I write you
    love notes,
The dark place that has gathered more darkness
To itself, like the sky on an August afternoon before
The hammering rainstorm—that candle glows like the one
Placed beside the small child's favorite picture
In the playhouse her father has built for her, and which
She has made into a sanctuary of friends and spirits
That bring her the kind of safety that sitting
In your favorite chair in your favorite room gives.

The passage of time since you left should have softened
The dark, as when an unwanted visitor comes for dinner
And throughout the draining evening you endure it,
Paying special attention to the food on your plate,
To the conversation you have no interest in, to the clean up,
Eating slowly so as to be able to swallow, and finding
When it's over and he's gone you can rest, greatly
    appreciating
The pleasure of climbing the steps to your room alone—but
This time he doesn't leave, stays on indefinitely like a
    boarder.

Before the rain, the sun is like a forty-watt bulb
Held behind sheets laundered so many times that their
    whiteness
Is lost and they've faded to gray, fails to brighten
The north windows, and the dullness of accommodated grief
Pervades everything. The rocker is still, the couch empty.
The carpet lays flat in the pattern of defeat. Our cat,
Crying at the door, follows me to my chair after I let him in
And works hard with his head and nursing paws to
    gather me in.

cooler
after rain—
dripping peonies

———∞———

cooler after rain
hairs on my arms
stand up

———∞———

standing at the edge
loud splash of the feeding carp—
my heart in my mouth

SHORT NOTES

I write short notes to myself
mostly on post-its or scraps;
soon they become talismans
close in my left breast pocket
or, lacking one, deep against
my thigh with coins and crystal,
a record of what I've set
my intent to, made precious
by the time I've done the thing.
Sometimes I like to save them,
the best ones put aside on
one of the altar places,
on top of the sock drawer
or beside the lamp on the
oak top bench by the front door.
Telling myself the story
of who I am all the time
begs interruption; these
reminders bring me pause.
Feeling a breath, a heartbeat,
memory passes over;
waters run over a rock,
clear in the sparkle of sun.

an eyeblink, a heartbeat
a breath—repeating—
that is all

---

after mowing
dew on the grass
and robins

---

slick soles
sandals getting wet
watering peppers

RACCOON

I caught a raccoon today darting in the trap
like the ones I let loose in your yard
and in the spirit of the day he came to me,
came right past the sleeping dog and crawled
onto my lap where my troubles lay, and nodded
his head as I told him the way you looked,
rain soaked with your nipples erect against
your black shirt, black hair all shining and wet
and dark eyes like twin smiles for those of us
who have sinned. The swing and sway and languor
of your walking hips. As he noticed I was telling
him of love that had the lust imparted to it in
sweet portions he cocked his thieving eye at me
before moving off, into the trees, into the woods
where things like acorns and foxes and ground-leaping
squirrels accompanied him under the ivy misted day.

I
What I have lost is not you.
It surprises me.
Here you are even as I hold you close
And I still feel it.
Like the ripple in your belly
When you talk with my hand on it.
Or the itchy place on your back.
I still weep to see the toy seal
He gave you for one of your birthdays.

Your lover calls you first thing
In the morning and all I feel
Is this dullness. The weeping
Arises from what I have lost
And it is not you, or my lover,
Or anything else I can put my hand on.

II
Wind up from the South
a little warmer, fresh
wisteria still green
after last night's rains
still I cannot get used
to living without my wife
it seems wrong that
she's not here with me
I sing a song of deep grief
and go on with my life
as best as I can

III
Now that November
has brought its gray skies
and dark afternoons,
with business failing
and the best friends
mirroring worry and care,
you gone, you say there's
no place for you here,
I am again alone
and don't like my company.
I am a failure.
There is nowhere to go.

PLUTO SQUARE SATURN

my nerve endings feel
as if they've been seared
the presence of others
beats on me like mallet blows
I have no memory no wonderment
no humor no interest no speech
flames of self-aversion lick at my heels
my fists clench and release
my palms are sweating, hot
affection turns to its opposite automatically
my beloved wears a care-worn face
I sleep fitfully and wake up
to nagging voices
something moves in slow circles
like a fish turning in the depths
I lay myself at the feet
of my best memories
and wait

forging ahead
who cares if they're lousy
these poems

———∞———

like a thousand eyes
the light green centers of
begonia leaves

———∞———

the leaves have fallen
the ash tree branches are bare
now I see the birds

What pleasure in the rhythm of her walk
A breath of wind, her dress a moving veil
She descends the stairway step by step
Her dress clings to her body in the heat
I love the way her hand rests on her face
She takes her hair against her open lips
My finger on my lip, the smell of earth
Now I rub the edges of my book
Her hair sweeps back in waves of brown and gold
A sign from ancient Egypt at her throat
Slow switching of her legs from side to side
I think about the seat she's sitting on
I've dreamed this dream of cleavages before
I want to put my face between her breasts
We move off to a place beneath the trees
We lie alone now, not a thing to say
She brings her legs around my waiting leg
She rubs her furry place against my thigh

An ancient rhythm in her movements now
I move my hands along her buttocks crease
I dare to put my finger in her ass
The scent of horses coming in the east
She moves in closer, gasping at my neck
Fishes swimming outside must have known
I turn her body over on her back
The mountain ash before its berries come
I move my tongue along her inner cleft
Branches filter starlight down below
My tongue finds sweetness underneath the salt
The treefrogs and the pondfrogs croak and wail
Hardness in me hardens harder still
We're spilling over in each other now
Outside of time, the thrumming bass note sounds

THE LAST PLACE

The last place I expected to find you
in back of this kitchen drawer
among the old parts to the cappuccino
machine not used for years; there
the special bottlecap you bought
when we still drank wine, there,
unused, the yellow rubber-ma-jig
that opens stuck lids with a twist
of the wrist.

                    I hold your image
in the palm of my heart, rock it
gently in the heart's arms, caress
its shining face with the heart's lips,
breathe the heart's breath across its brow.

The song the heart sings soothes
everything for miles around, crooning
and cooing like celestial Frank Sinatra,
only the heart's the bandleader,
singer, microphone, audience and hall;
you're in my heart's core, darling, that's all.

BIRD CALL

I have heard
the returning nuthatches
on the first cool morning
after weeks of debilitating heat.
The air has cleared; the sky
is bright blue; we breathe easier.
I slept well, and, for the first time
in weeks my head is clearing.
As I watch the brilliant sunlight
turn the deep green African violet leaves
silvery, a crow flies overhead,
destination unknown. So much
of the world—almost all—continues
without my recognition, Yet
the catbird seems to be calling me:
"Pay attention; you have a part
in this," he says. Bright red berries
hang now in clusters
from the mountain ash.
How lovely the light is.

General Hsiu's head is shaved bald as a monk,
His sweeping brows arch toward the gleaming
Dome above blazing eyes. He holds back in love,
Not in battle, this fierce one. Who was his wife,
His lover? Where are they now if not dead
Beneath the rubble of earth? Alone at the end
Of his life he finds solace wandering the barren
Plains, loves then his horse, the open air, sun,
Wind and stars. He remembers her most before
The infrequent rain, his heart grows heavy and
His loins ache but always the call to move onward
Claims him. On the day of his death he recalls
A small detail—the peach-fuzz hairs on the inside
Rim of her ear—and in place of the stab of longing
He hears a whisper in the darkness from darkness.